Alfred's Basic Piano L[...]

Piano

Fun Book
Complete Level 1

A COLLECTION OF 55 ENTERTAINING SOLOS

FUN BOOK, Complete Level 1, of Alfred's Basic Piano Library contains 55 short pieces, carefully coordinated PAGE BY PAGE with the material in LESSON BOOK, Complete Level 1. These are, for the most part, shorter and easier than the pieces in RECITAL BOOK, Complete Level 1. They may be used in addition to or instead of the pieces in the recital book. These pieces serve to make the course more flexible and more easily adaptable to the taste and needs of the individual student. They may be used to provide additional reinforcement to the concepts each contains as well as extra reading material at the proper level of advancement.

This book also answers the often expressed need for a variety of supplementary material for use when two or more students from the same family are studying the same course and prefer not to play exactly the same pieces.

The subjects for the selections in this book were often suggested by students and teachers, with a view to adding good humor and amusement to the lesson. It is our hope that this book will live up to its name, for teachers and students alike.

Willard A. Palmer ◆ Morton Manus ◆ Amanda Vick Lethco

Alfred Music
P.O. Box 10003
Van Nuys, CA 91410-0003
alfred.com

Second Edition
Copyright © MCMXCVI by Alfred Music
All rights reserved. Produced in USA.

ISBN-10: 0-7390-2199-0
ISBN-13: 978-0-7390-2199-6

Contents

Use after BATTER UP,
Complete LESSON BOOK 1 (page 9).

Dyno, My Pet Dinosaur

Suggestion: When repeating, you may move the hands to a lower position (with thumbs on a lower C),
if you wish. This will sound more like a dinosaur.

4

Use after THE SKI LIFT (page 11).

MIDDLE C POSITION

Fuzzy Wuzzy

Brightly

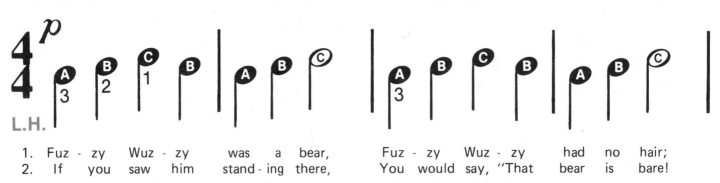

1. Fuz - zy Wuz - zy was a bear, Fuz - zy Wuz - zy had no hair;
2. If you saw him stand - ing there, You would say, "That bear is bare!

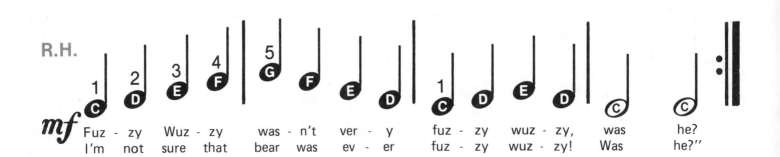

Fuz - zy Wuz - zy was - n't ver - y fuz - zy wuz - zy, was he?
I'm not sure that bear was ev - er fuz - zy wuz - zy! Was he?"

Use after RAIN, RAIN! (page 13).

Circus Day!

Happily

f

2nd time play ONE OCTAVE (8 notes) LOWER

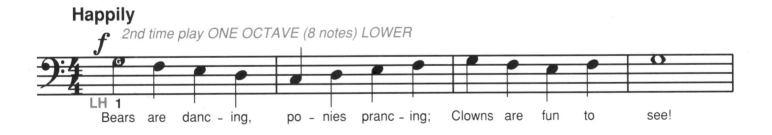

LH 1

Bears are danc - ing, po - nies pranc - ing; Clowns are fun to see!

1

When the cir - cus comes to town, What fun for you and me!

6

Use after A HAPPY SONG (page 15).

Up to the Moon!

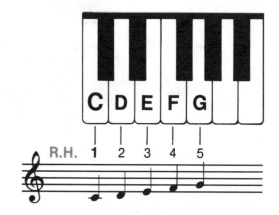

Moderately fast

f If I had a rock - et, I might fly up to the moon!

p I would need two rock - ets, 'cause I'd come back home real soon!

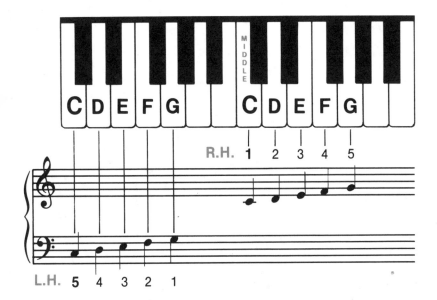

Row, Row, Row Your Boat

(RIGHT SIDE UP AND UPSIDE DOWN)

The 1st line is the familiar tune.
The 2nd line is the same, upside-down!

C POSITION

Moderately slow

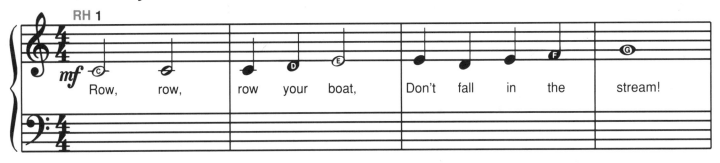

RH 1

mf Row, row, row your boat, Don't fall in the stream!

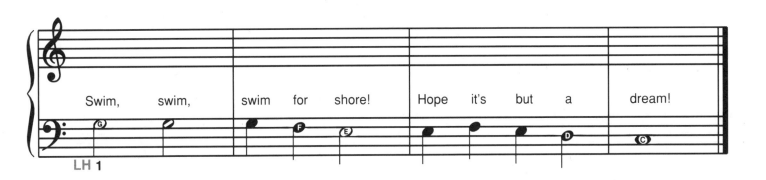

Swim, swim, swim for shore! Hope it's but a dream!

LH 1

8

Use after "POSITION C" (page 17).

Figure Skating

C POSITION

Cautiously

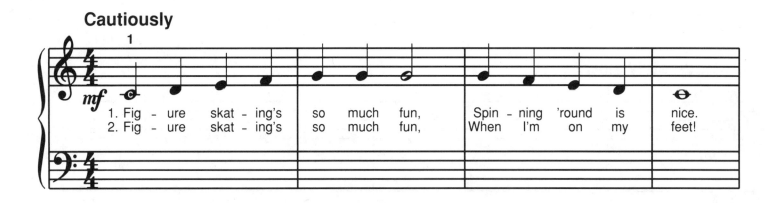

1. Fig – ure skat – ing's so much fun, Spin – ning 'round is nice.
2. Fig – ure skat – ing's so much fun, When I'm on my feet!

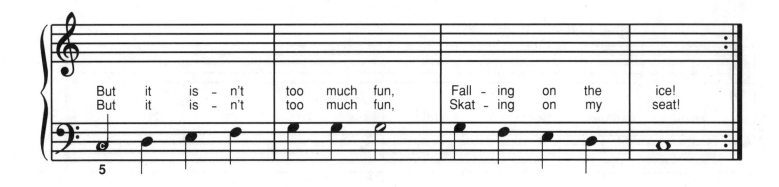

But it is – n't too much fun, Fall – ing on the ice!
But it is – n't too much fun, Skat – ing on my seat!

Use after JUST A SECOND! (page 18).

Gliding

Moderately slow

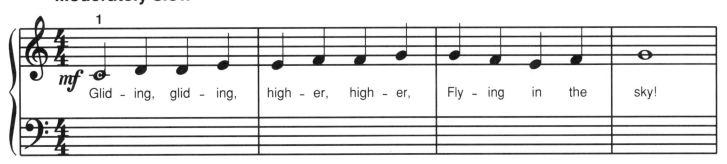

mf Glid - ing, glid - ing, high - er, high - er, Fly - ing in the sky!

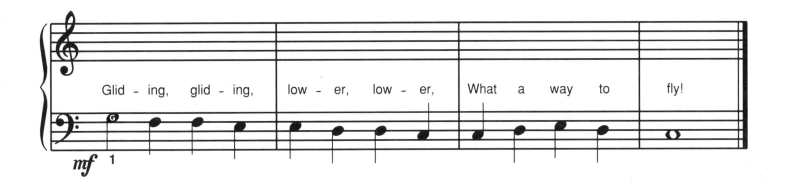

Glid - ing, glid - ing, low - er, low - er, What a way to fly!

mf

Use after SAILING (page 19).

Strange Lands

Moderately slow

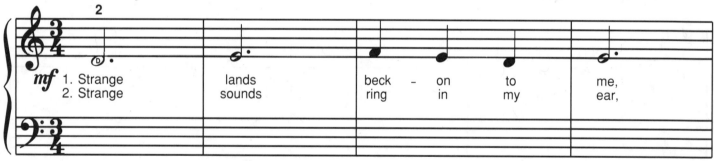

mf
1. Strange lands beck – on to me,
2. Strange sounds ring in to my ear,

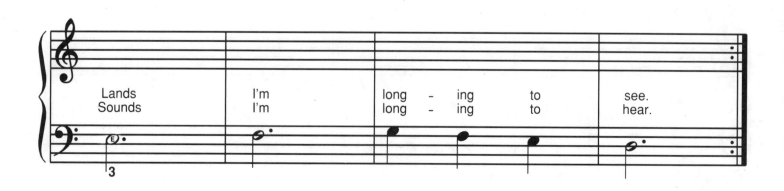

Lands I'm long – ing to see.
Sounds I'm long – ing to hear.

Biking

Use after WISHING WELL (page 20).

Slow

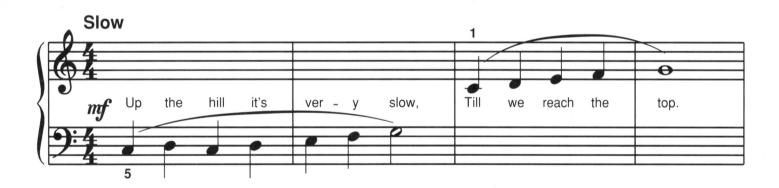

Up the hill it's ver - y slow, Till we reach the top.

Faster   **Gradually slower**

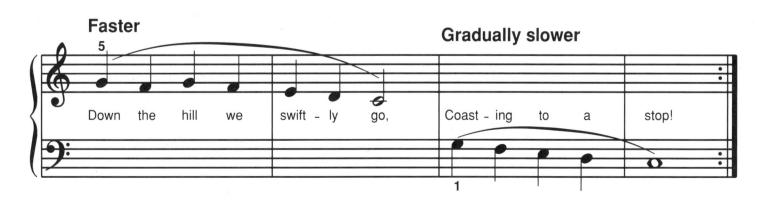

Down the hill we swift - ly go, Coast - ing to a stop!

Use after BALLOONS (page 21).

On a Funny, Sunny Day

Happily

1. On a fun – ny, sun – ny day, Oh, what fun to run and play!
2. In the shin – ing morn – ing sun, We can have a lot of fun!

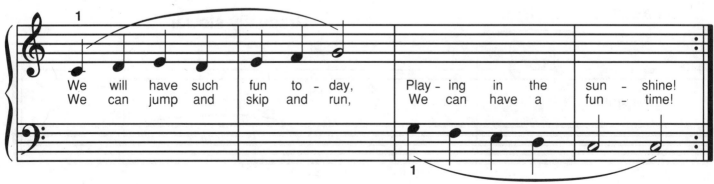

We will have such fun to – day, Play – ing in the sun – shine!
We can jump and skip and run, We can have a fun – time!

Use after WHO'S ON THIRD? (page 22).

Just for Fun!

Moderately fast

2nd time BOTH HANDS 8va (ONE OCTAVE HIGHER)

1. What can I do? What can you do? Just for fun, just for fun.
2. What can I play? What can you play? Just for fun, just for fun.

What can we do? What can we do? Just to have some fun.
What can we play? What can we play? Just to have some fun.

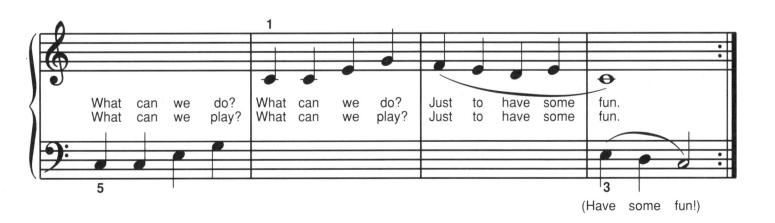

(Have some fun!)

Use after MEXICAN HAT DANCE (page 23).

Trolley Song

Happily!

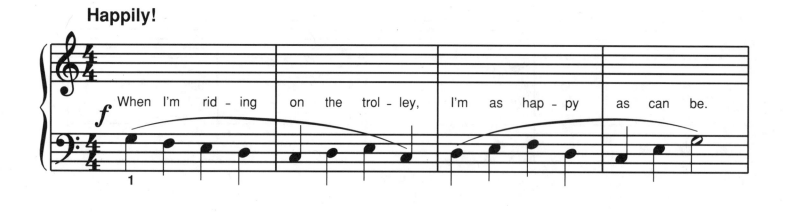

When I'm rid – ing on the trol – ley, I'm as hap – py as can be.

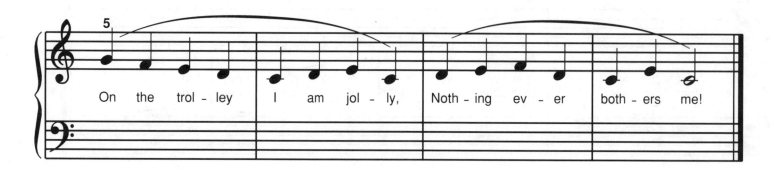

On the trol – ley I am jol – ly, Noth – ing ev – er both – ers me!

Use after ROCK SONG (page 25).

Rockin' & Rollin'

Brightly

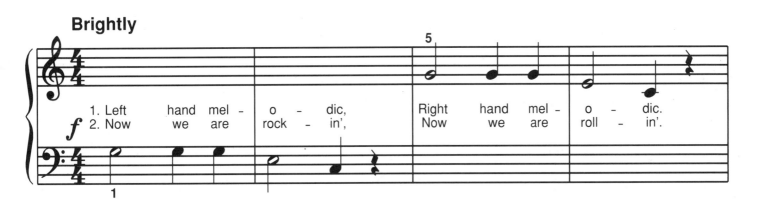

1. Left hand mel – o – dic, Right hand mel – o – dic.
2. Now we are rock – in', Now we are roll – in'.

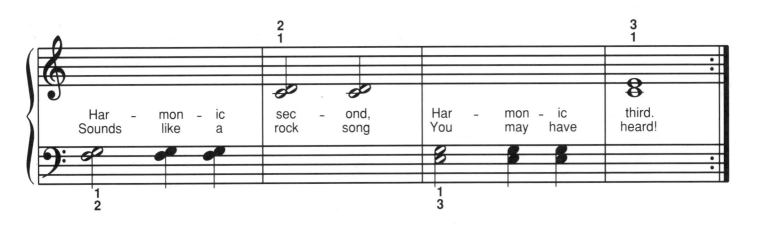

Har – mon – ic sec – ond, Har – mon – ic third.
Sounds like a rock song You may have heard!

Use after ROCKETS (page 26).

If I Won Ten Million Dollars

Moderately fast

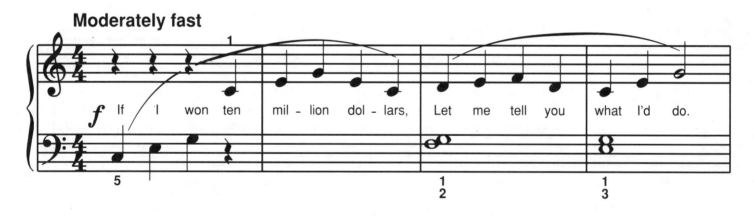

f If I won ten mil – lion dol – lars, Let me tell you what I'd do.

BOTH HANDS 8va (ONE OCTAVE HIGHER)

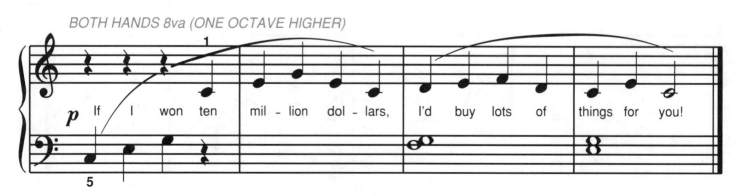

p If I won ten mil – lion dol – lars, I'd buy lots of things for you!

Use after SEA DIVERS (page 27).

Where Did You Get That Hat?

Happily

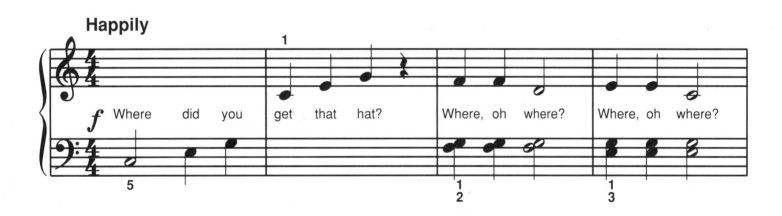

Where did you get that hat? Where, oh where? Where, oh where?

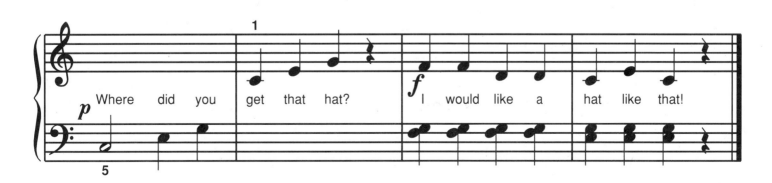

Where did you get that hat? I would like a hat like that!

18

Use after LOVE SOMEBODY (page 29).

Showstopper!

Moderately fast, with a steady beat

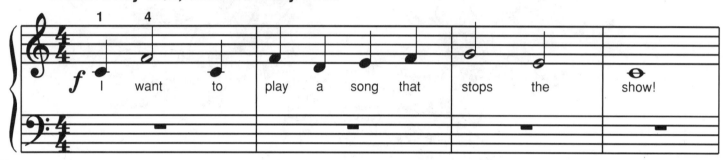

I want to play a song that stops the show!

That's just be - cause I want to hear some ap - plause.

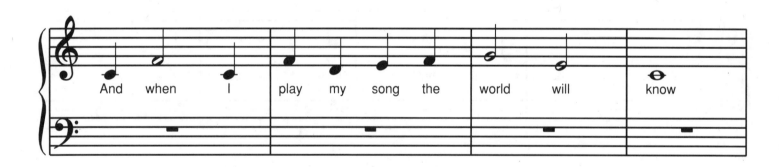

And when I play my song the world will know

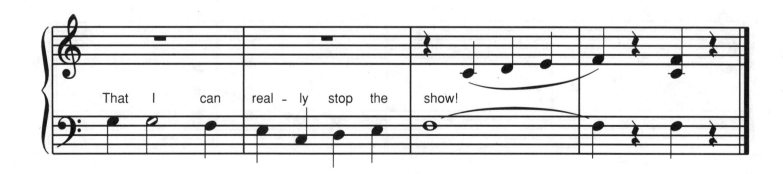

That I can real - ly stop the show!

Use after MY FIFTH (page 30).

What Can I Share?

Moderately slow

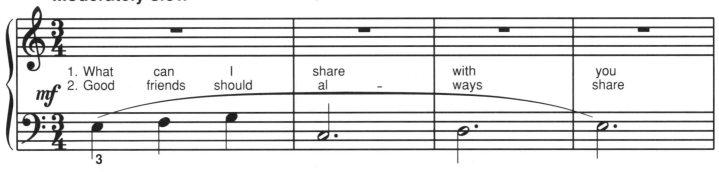

1. What can I share with you
2. Good friends I should al - ways share

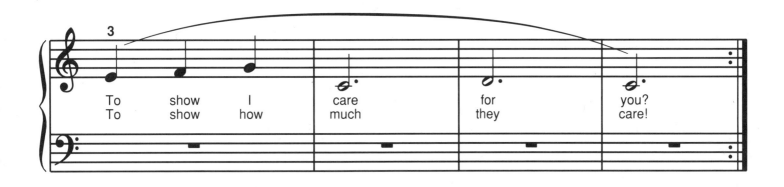

To show I care for you?
To show how much they care!

Use after MY FIFTH (page 30).

Rock Along!

Moderately fast

f Play thirds and fifths, and we'll rock a - long!

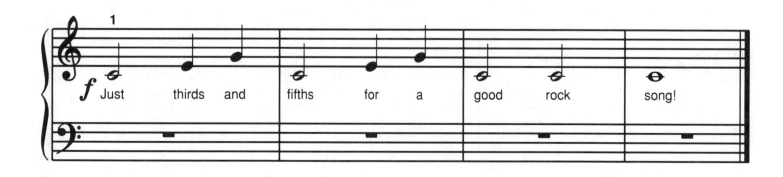

f Just thirds and fifths for a good rock song!

Use after THE DONKEY (page 31).

What Will You Do?

Name all the HARMONIC INTERVALS in this piece before you play it.

Brightly

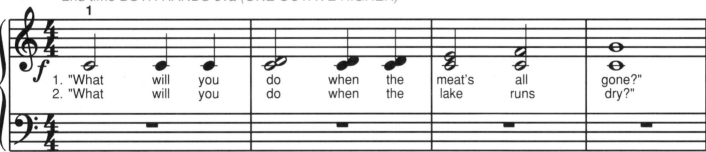

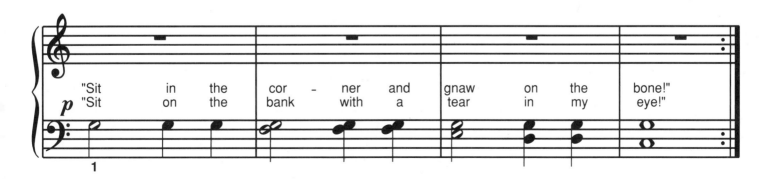

The Big Parade

Use after THE DONKEY (page 31).

Fast march tempo

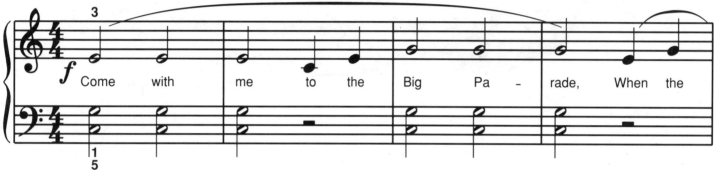

Come with me to the Big Pa - rade, When the

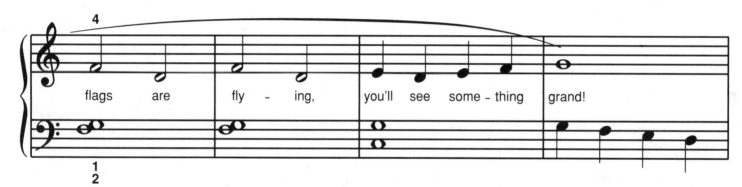

flags are fly - ing, you'll see some - thing grand!

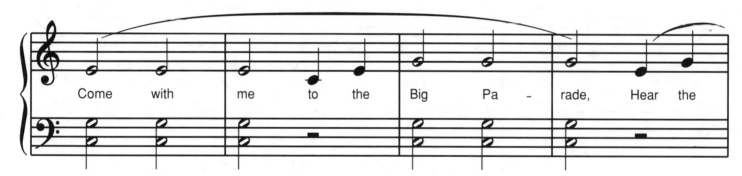

Come with me to the Big Pa - rade, Hear the

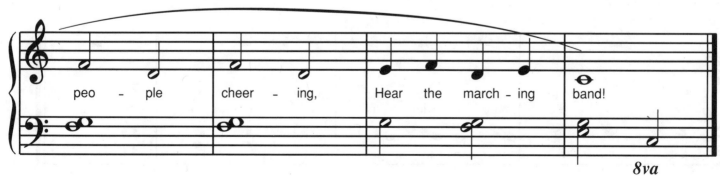

peo - ple cheer - ing, Hear the march - ing band!

8va
Play one octave lower

Use after THE DONKEY (page 31).

Sun's Up!

Brightly

2nd time BOTH HANDS 8va (ONE OCTAVE HIGHER)

1. Sun's   up!   Sun's   up!
2. Sun's   up!   Sun's   up!

What   a   beau - ti - ful   day!
Come   and   join   in   the   fun!

Sun's   up!   Sun's   up!
Sun's   up!   Sun's   up!

Let's   all   go   out   and   play!
Come   and   play   in   the   Sun!

Use after PLAYING IN G POSITION (page 32).

"Moon-Walk"

G POSITION

Moderately slow

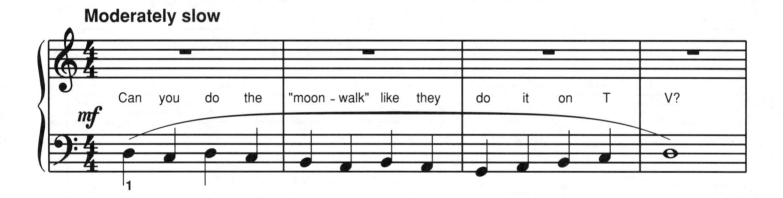

mf

Can you do the "moon - walk" like they do it on T V?

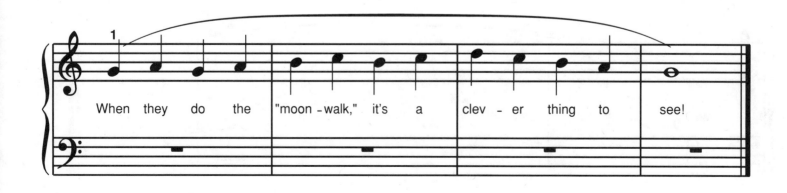

When they do the "moon - walk," it's a clev - er thing to see!

Old Woman

Use after JINGLE BELLS! (page 33).

G POSITION

Folk song

Moderately fast

26

Use after A FRIEND LIKE YOU (page 34).

The Tuba and the Piccolo

Moderately

2nd time play L.H. ONE OCTAVE LOWER
and R.H. ONE OCTAVE HIGHER

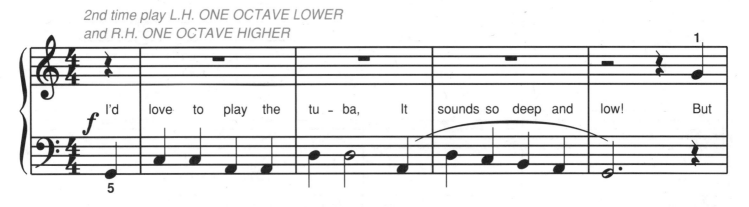

I'd love to play the tu-ba, It sounds so deep and low! But

when I want some high notes, I'll take the pic - co - lo!

Use after HORSE SENSE (page 35).

Amadeus

C POSITION REVIEW

Based on a melody by
Wolfgang Amadeus Mozart

*Go back to 𝄆 and play again.

If I Had a Pony!

Use after HORSE SENSE (page 35).

Brightly

If I had a po – ny I'd gal – lop a – way! I'd

jump on my po – ny and ride him all day!

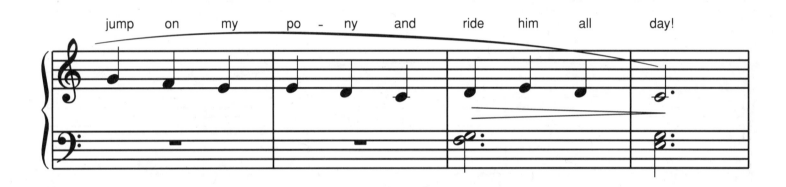

Gal – lop – ing, gal – lop – ing, gal – lop – ing, gal – lop – ing,

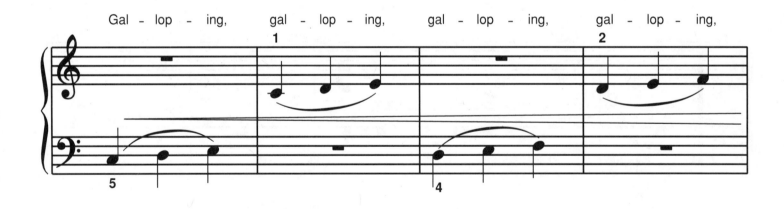

Gal – lop – ing, rid – ing my po – ny all day!

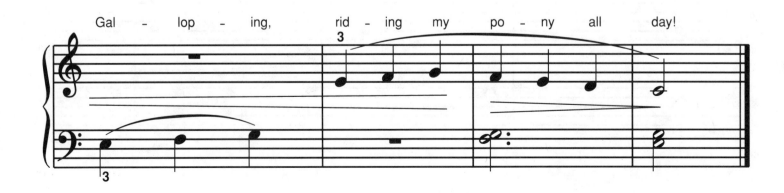

Use after MY ROBOT (page 36).

Boogie-Woogie Beat

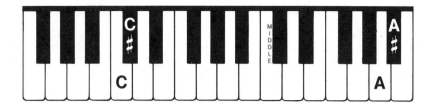

G POSITION

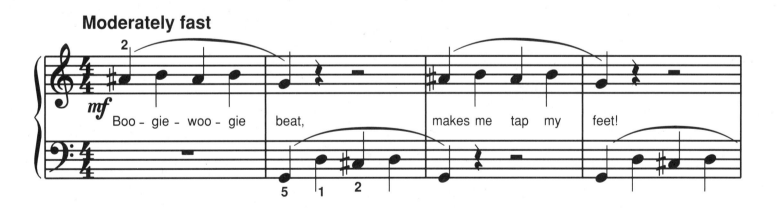

Moderately fast

mf

Boo - gie - woo - gie beat,   makes me tap my feet!

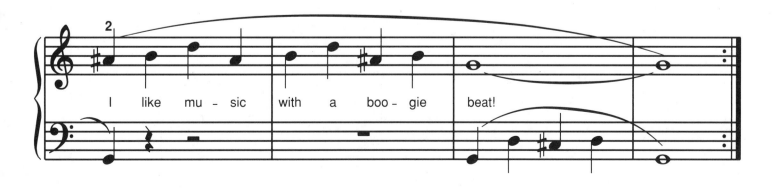

I like mu - sic with a boo - gie beat!

30

Will You, Won't You?

Use after MONEY CAN'T BUY EV'RYTHING! (page 37).

Adapted from "Alice in Wonderland,"
by Lewis Carroll

Moderately fast

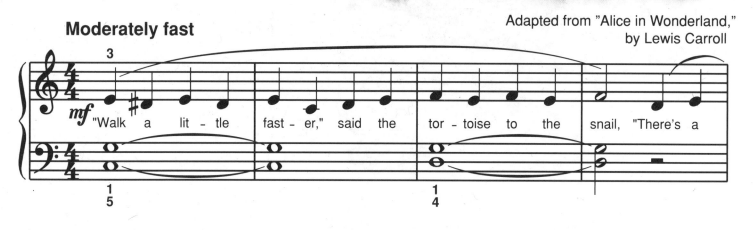

"Walk a lit-tle fast-er," said the tor-toise to the snail, "There's a

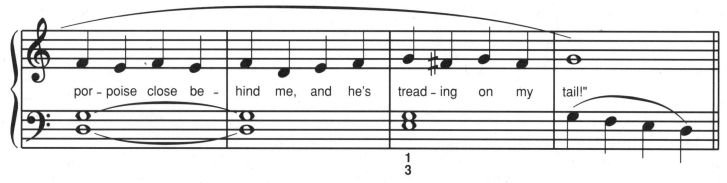

por-poise close be-hind me, and he's tread-ing on my tail!"

A little faster, very rhythmically

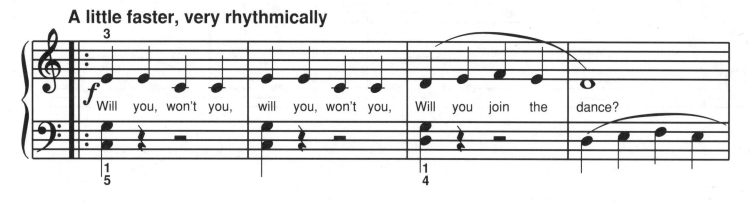

Will you, won't you, will you, won't you, Will you join the dance?

Will you, won't you, will you, won't you, Won't you join the dance?

Use after MONEY CAN'T BUY EV'RYTHING! (page 37).

Surprise!

Happily

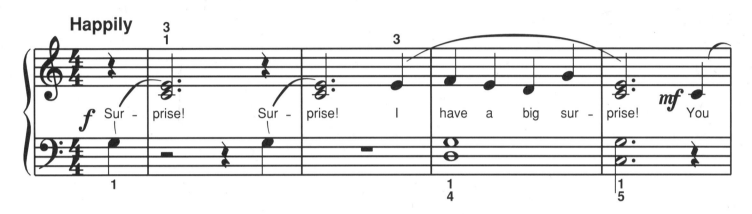

Sur - prise! Sur - prise! I have a big sur - prise! You

need - n't hold your hands out, You need - n't close your eyes. Sur - prise! Sur -

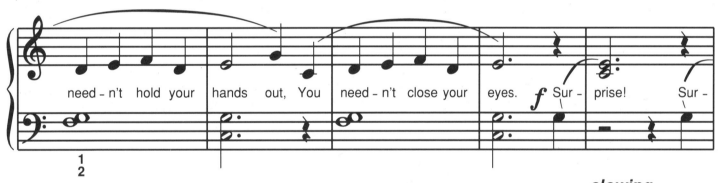

prise! This won't take ver - y long; The big sur - prise is sim - ply this:

slowing _ _ _

faster
Both hands one octave lower

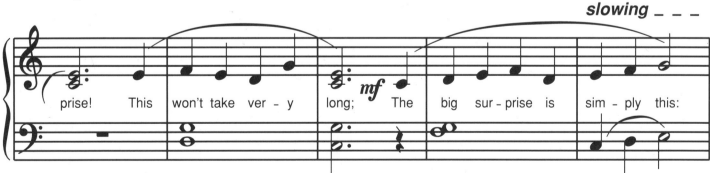

(spoken)

I've learned to play this song! Sur - prise!

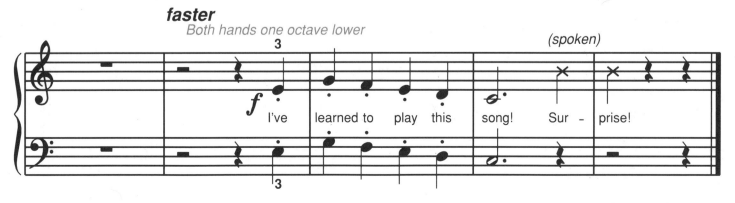

Anywhere You Rock!

Use after ROCKIN' TUNE (page 38).

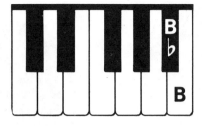

B♭ and A♯ are the
SAME BLACK KEY!

Moderate rock tempo

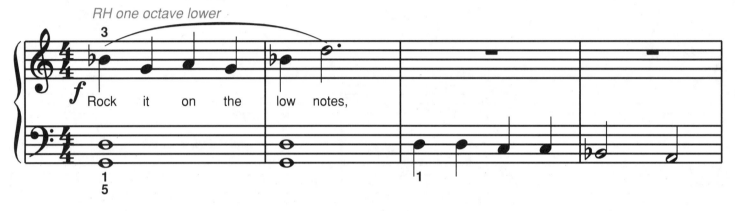

Rock it on the low notes,

Rock it in the mid - dle,

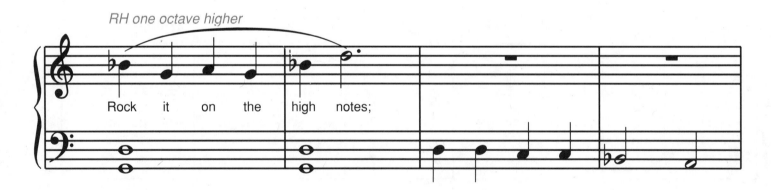

Rock it on the high notes;

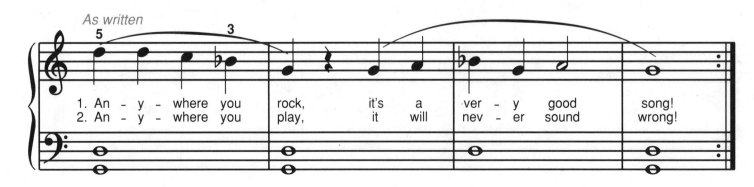

1. An - y - where you rock, it's a ver - y good song!
2. An - y - where you play, it will nev - er sound wrong!

Musette

A *MUSETTE* is a small French bagpipe.

The title "Musette" is often given to dances that were accompanied by such an instrument.

Brightly

The RH may be played 8va (ONE OCTAVE HIGHER) 2nd time.

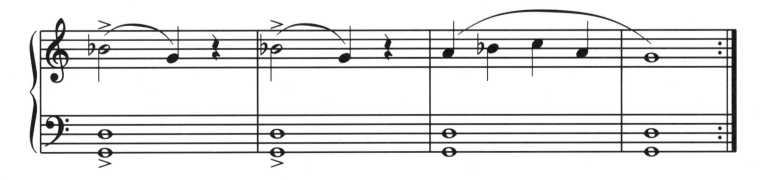

Use after THE CLOWN (page 39).

Theme from
Tchaikowsky's
4th Symphony

P. I. Tchaikowsky

Use after THE CLOWN (page 39).

Für Ludwig*

Not too fast, but with great optimism

If I prac-tice well, some-day you'll hear me

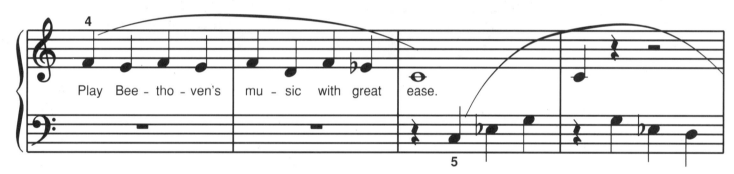

Play Bee-tho-ven's mu-sic with great ease.

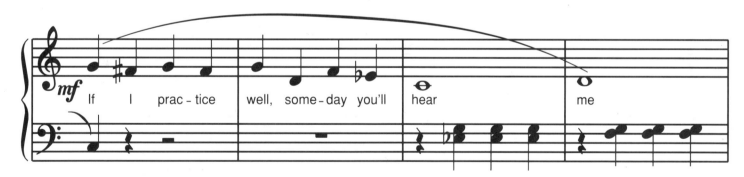

If I prac-tice well, some-day you'll hear me

Play that mu-sic he wrote for E - lise.

*Ludwig van Beethoven – Composer of *Für Elise* (For Elise).

8va

Cracker Jack!

Use after RAINDROPS (page 40).

Fast polka tempo

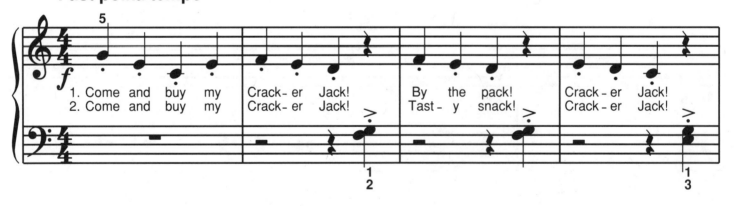

1. Come and buy my Crack- er Jack! By the pack! Crack- er Jack!
2. Come and buy my Crack- er Jack! Tast- y snack! Crack- er Jack!

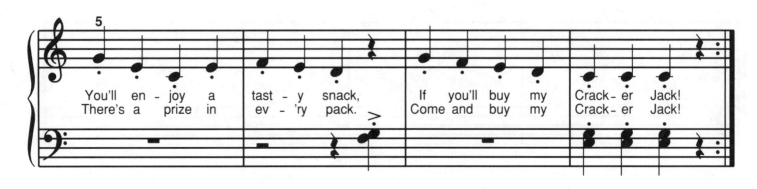

You'll en- joy a tast- y snack, If you'll buy my Crack- er Jack!
There's a prize in ev- 'ry pack. Come and buy my Crack- er Jack!

Use after RAINDROPS (page 40).

The Fish Won't Bite

Brightly

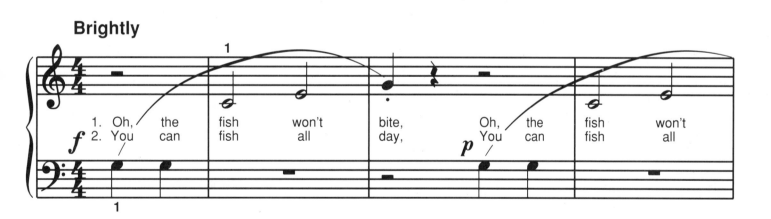

1. Oh, the fish won't bite, Oh, the fish won't
2. You can fish fish all day, You can fish fish all

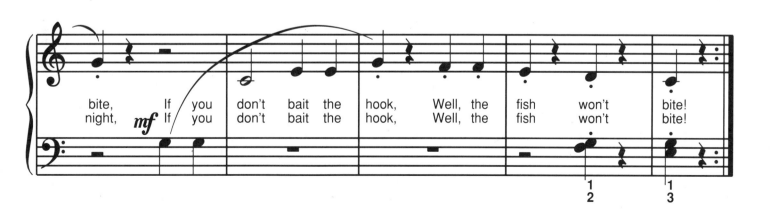

bite, If you don't bait the hook, Well, the fish won't bite!
night, If you don't bait the hook, Well, the fish won't bite!

Knock, Knock!

Use after WHEN THE SAINTS GO MARCHING IN (page 41).

Moderately fast

Knock, knock! Who's there? Wen – dy! Wen – dy who?

"Wen – dy Saints Go March – ing In!" That's an aw – ful joke. Ha ha!

Knock, knock! Who's there? Man – ny! Man – ny who?

"Man – ny can't buy ev – 'ry – thing!" That's an aw – ful joke. Ha – ha!

If you'd like to play this game again, here's more:

Knock, knock! Who's there?	Knock, knock! Who's there?
Boo— ! Boo– who?	Wanda! Wanda who?
Didn't mean to make you cry!	"Wanda where the money goes!"
That's an awful joke. Ha-ha!	That's an awful joke. Ha-ha!

A Prayer for Peace

Use after WALTZ TIME (page 43).

MIDDLE C POSITION

Andante moderato

1. Let us say a prayer for peace all a - round the world.
2. Let us pray that strife will cease all a - round the world.

mf Come and join us in our prayer for all peo - ple ev - 'ry - where,

"Fa - ther, keep us in Thy care, all a - round the world!"

A - men, A - men, A - men, A - men.

The Purple Cow*

Use after THE RAINBOW (page 45).

Allegro moderato

Words by Gelett Burgess

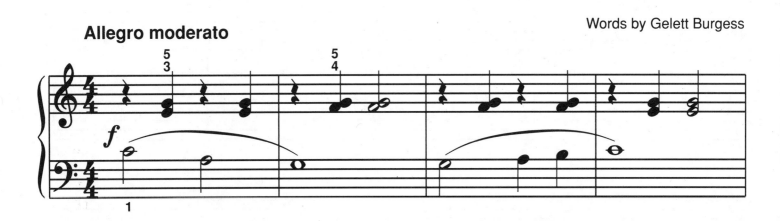

*This is the best known poem by Gelett Burgess, who later wrote the following:

> Ah, yes! I wrote "The Purple Cow,"
> I'm sorry now I wrote it.
> But I can tell you anyhow,
> I'll kill you if you quote it!

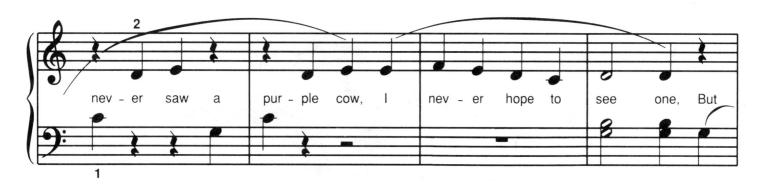

never saw a purple cow, I never hope to see one, But

gradually slower to

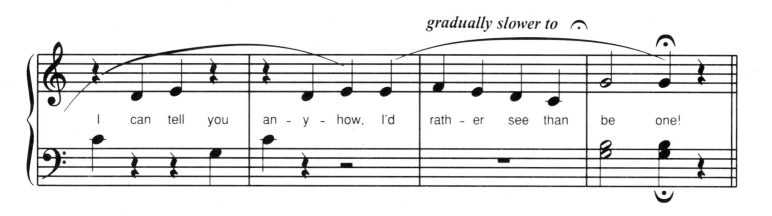

I can tell you an-y-how, I'd rather see than be one!

resume original tempo

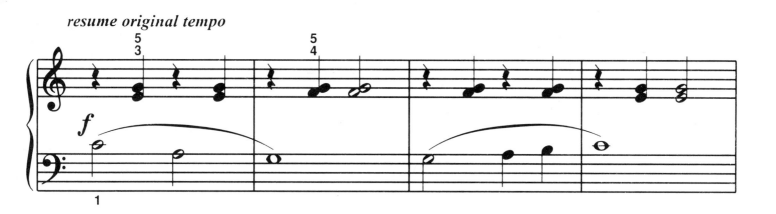

gradually slower to end

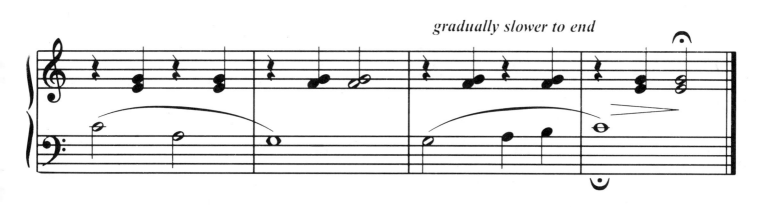

Whoopee Ti-Yi-Yo

Use after HAPPY BIRTHDAY TO YOU! (page 47).

Cowboy song

*A "dogie" is an orphaned calf. The first syllable, "do," rhymes with "go."

Use after INDIANS (page 50).

Barrel of Monkeys!

G POSITION

Happily

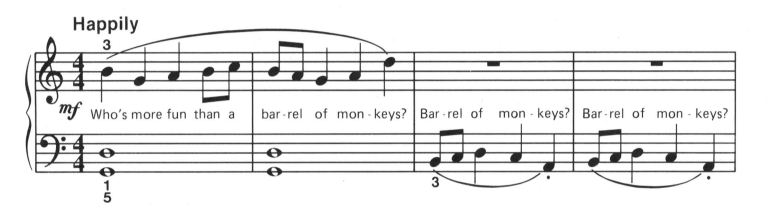

Who's more fun than a bar-rel of mon-keys? Bar-rel of mon-keys? Bar-rel of mon-keys?

Who's more fun than a bar-rel of mon-keys? Bar-rel of mon-keys? Bar-rel of mon-keys?

Both hands one octave higher — *Both hands two octaves higher* — *Both hands one octave lower*

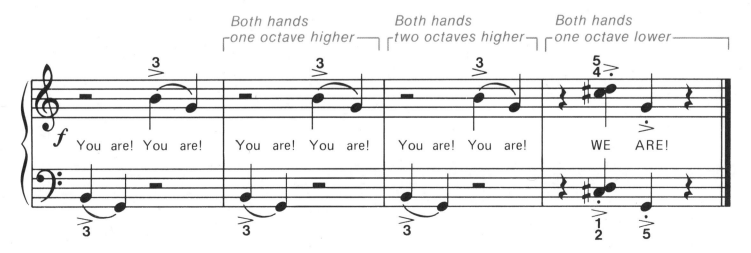

You are! You are! You are! You are! You are! You are! WE ARE!

44

Amigos

Use after NEW POSITION G (page 51).

Brightly

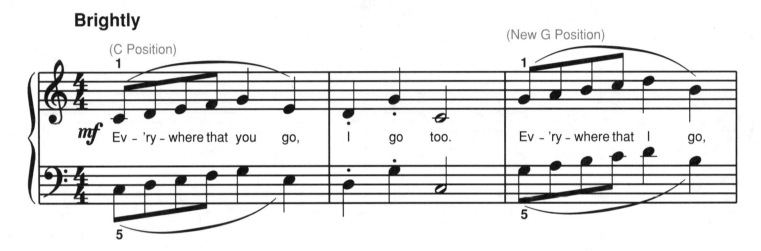

(C Position) (New G Position)

Ev-'ry-where that you go, I go too. Ev-'ry-where that I go,

Both hands one octave higher

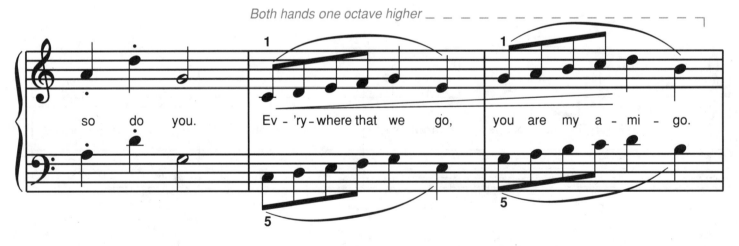

so do you. Ev-'ry-where that we go, you are my a-mi-go.

Both hands one octave lower

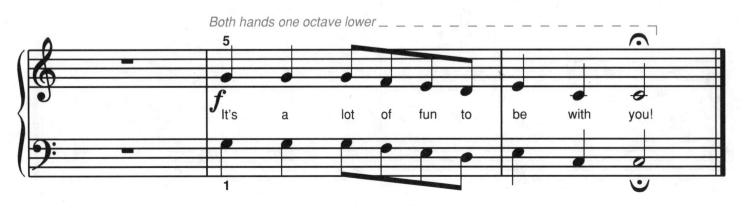

It's a lot of fun to be with you!

Use after HARP SONG (page 53)
or CONCERT TIME (page 54).

Who Did?

NEW G POSITION

Brightly

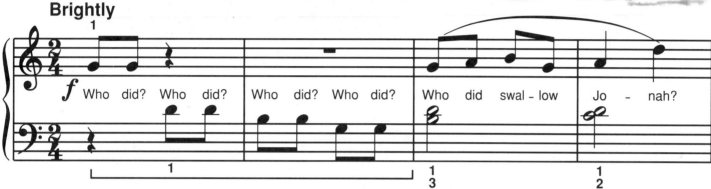

Who did? Who did? Who did? Who did? Who did swal-low Jo - nah?

Both hands one octave lower

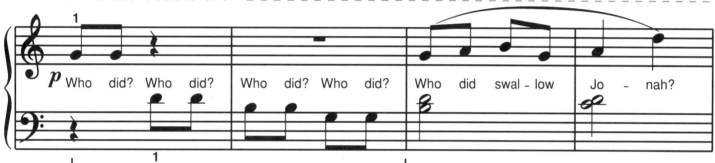

Who did? Who did? Who did? Who did? Who did swal-low Jo - nah?

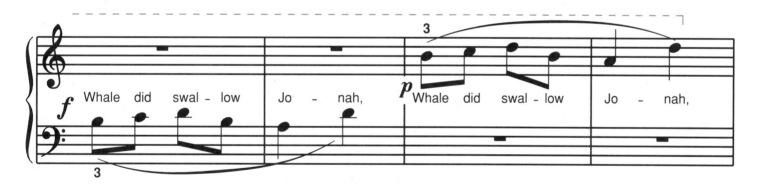

Whale did swal-low Jo - nah, Whale did swal-low Jo - nah,

(Both hands as written)

Whale did swal-low Jo - nah down!

If you'd like to play it twice, here's another verse:

Who did? Who did? Who did? Who did?
Who found little Moses? *(etc.)*

Pharaoh's daughter found him, Found him in the water,
Pharaoh's daughter found him there!

Can't Get 'Em Up!

Use after MUSIC BOX ROCK (page 55).

Military bugle call

Allegro

We can't get 'em up, we can't get 'em up, we can't get 'em up this morn - ing! We

can't get 'em up, we can't get 'em up, we can't get 'em up to - day!

ritardando

We can't get 'em up to - day!

Use after THE MAGIC MAN (page 56).

Music with a Beat

Rock tempo

RH one octave lower; 2nd time, as written

1. Mu - sic with a beat   Makes me tap my
2. Mu - sic with a beat   Makes me feel so

feet!   That's why I like   mu - sic with a
neat!

Repeat as many times as you wish, softer and softer.

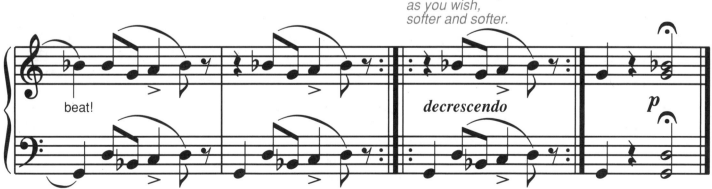

beat!   *decrescendo*

Boogie-Woogie Goose

Use after THE MAGIC MAN (page 56).

Allegro moderato

Go tell Aunt Rho - die,   Go tell Aunt

Rho - die,   Go tell Aunt Rho - die

*Pairs of eighth notes may be played a bit unevenly, in a "lilting" style:

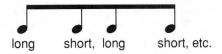

long   short, long   short, etc.

her goose is – n't dead.

It's do – in' the boo – gie, It's do – in' the

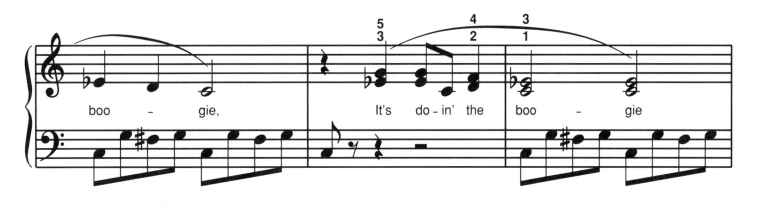

boo – gie, It's do – in' the boo – gie

in her flow – er bed! *ritardando*

Ain't Gonna Rain

Use after THE GREATEST SHOW ON EARTH! (page 58).

MIDDLE D POSITION

Allegro moderato

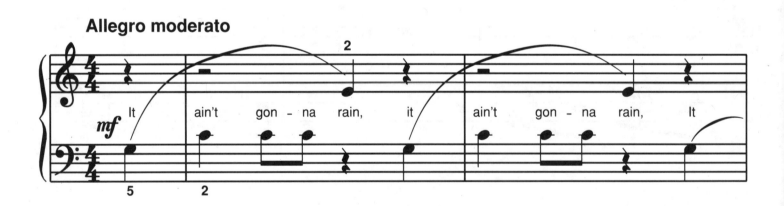

It ain't gon - na rain, it ain't gon - na rain, It

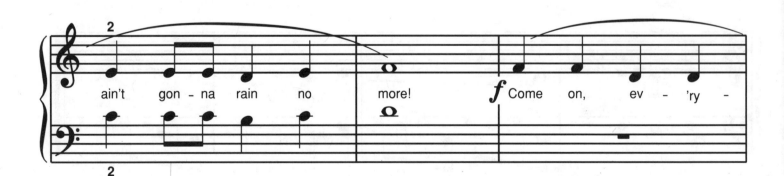

ain't gon - na rain no more! Come on, ev - 'ry -

bod – y sing, Ain't gon – na rain no more!

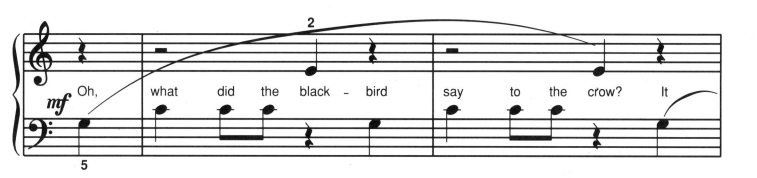

mf Oh, what did the black – bird say to the crow? It

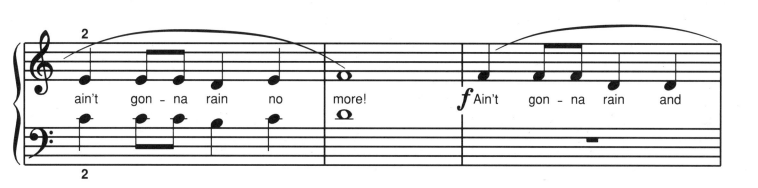

ain't gon – na rain no more! *f* Ain't gon – na rain and

ain't gon – na snow, Ain't gon – na rain no more!

52

Get Away!

Use after THE GREATEST SHOW ON EARTH! (page 58).

This piece uses both the **MIDDLE C POSITION** and the **MIDDLE D POSITION**.

Adapted from themes from
the Overture to "William Tell,"
by G. Rossini

MIDDLE C POSITION

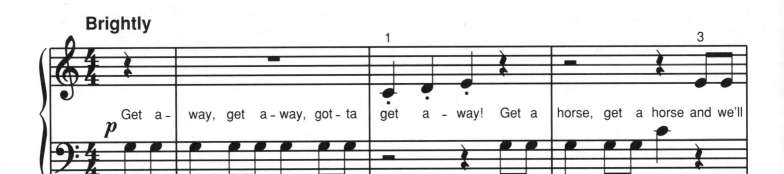

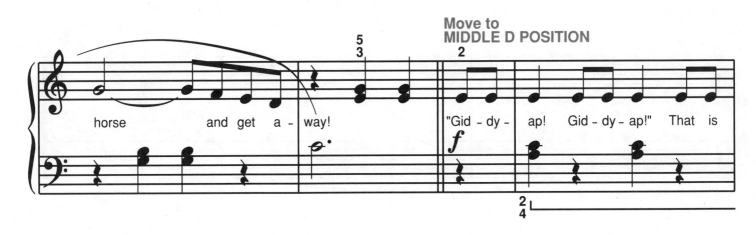

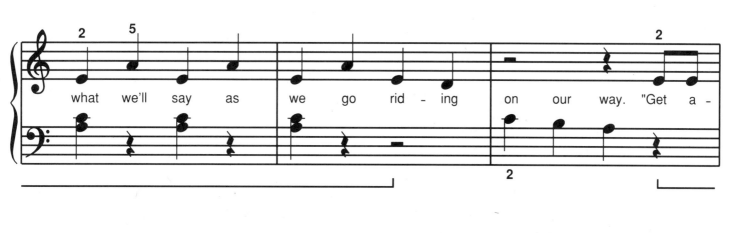

what we'll say as we go rid - ing on our way. "Get a -

long! Get a - long!" That - 'll be our song as we go gal - lop -

Move back to MIDDLE C POSITION

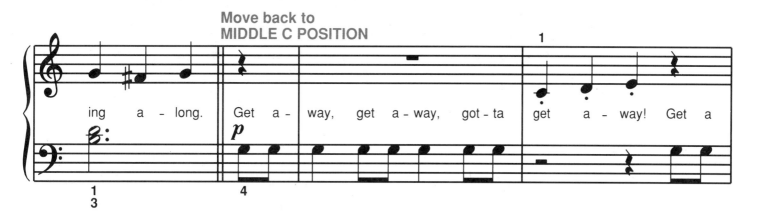

ing a - long. Get a - way, get a - way, got - ta get a - way! Get a

horse, get a horse and we'll ride all day! Get a - way, get a - way, got - ta

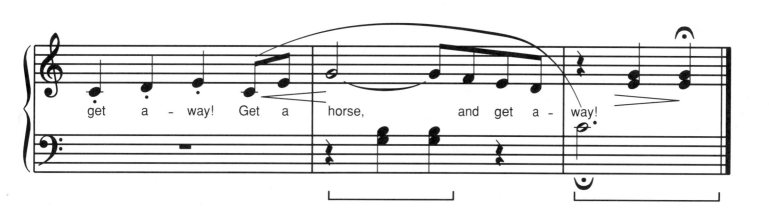

get a - way! Get a horse, and get a - way!

On With the Show!

Use after MEASURING HALF STEPS (page 60).

March tempo

On with the show! Strike up the band! Come on, let's go!

*Pairs of eighth notes may be played a bit unevenly, in a "lilting" style:

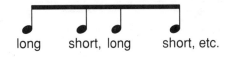

long   short, long   short, etc.

Give them a hand! Bring on the clowns, tum-blers and bears!

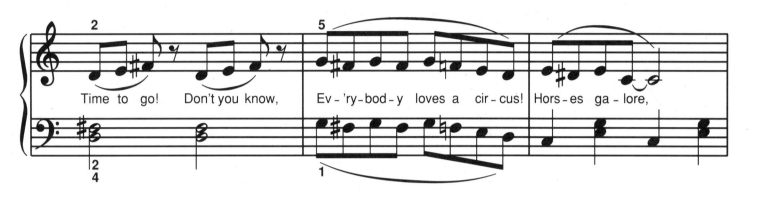

Time to go! Don't you know, Ev-'ry-bod-y loves a cir-cus! Hors-es ga-lore,

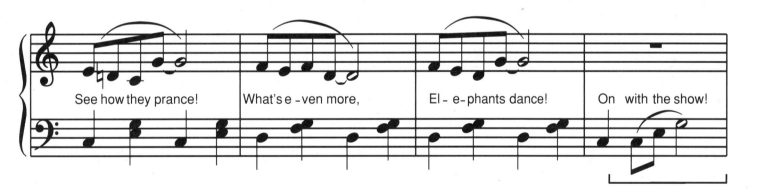

See how they prance! What's e-ven more, El-e-phants dance! On with the show!

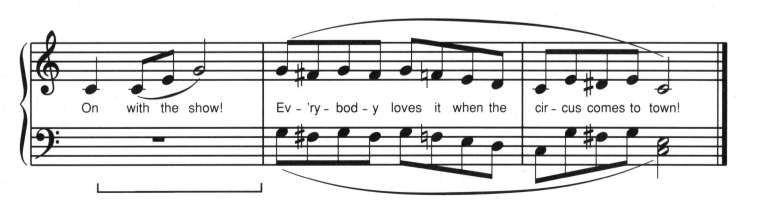

On with the show! Ev-'ry-bod-y loves it when the cir-cus comes to town!

The Howling Wind

Use after THE WHIRLWIND (page 61).

MIDDLE D "HALF-STEP" POSITION

Use after THE PLANETS (page 63).

God Made Them All

MIDDLE D "WHOLE-STEP" POSITION

Andante moderato

God made the earth, God made the sky,

God made the clouds that go drift - ing by.

God made the moon, God made the sun,

ritardando

God made the stars, ev - 'ry one!

Use after THE KEY OF G MAJOR (page 66).

Three Wise Monkeys

HAND POSITION: L.H. plays lower tetrachord,
R.H. plays upper tetrachord.

KEY OF G MAJOR
Key Signature: one sharp (F♯)

FOR MORE FUN: **Play also in C TETRACHORD POSITION (5's on C's one octave apart).**

Use after THE KEY OF G MAJOR (page 66).

The Brave Knight

HAND POSITION: L.H. plays lower tetrachord,
R.H. plays upper tetrachord.

KEY OF G MAJOR
Key Signature: one sharp (F♯)

Moderato

Tuf – fy was a no – ble – man, Tuf – fy was a knight;

Tuf – fy jumped up – on his horse and rode with all his might.

Tuf – fy rode out in – to the for – est one day;

There he saw a rab – bit and it fright – ened him a – way!

FOR MORE FUN: Play also in C TETRACHORD POSITION (5's on C's one octave apart).

60

Use after FRENCH LULLABY (page 67).

The Baseball Game

R.H. in C POSITION
L.H. in LOW G POSITION

March tempo

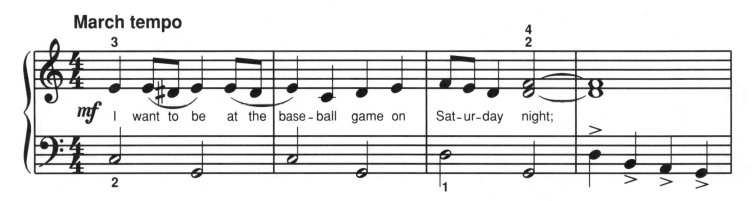

I want to be at the base-ball game on Sat-ur-day night;

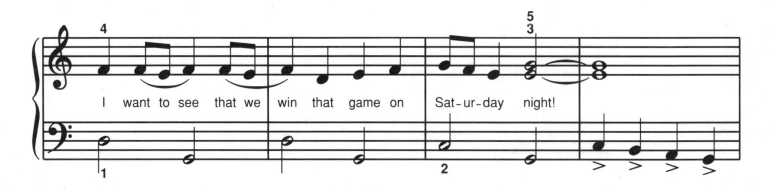

I want to see that we win that game on Sat-ur-day night!

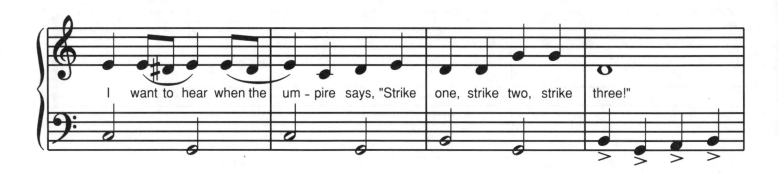

I want to hear when the um-pire says, "Strike one, strike two, strike three!"

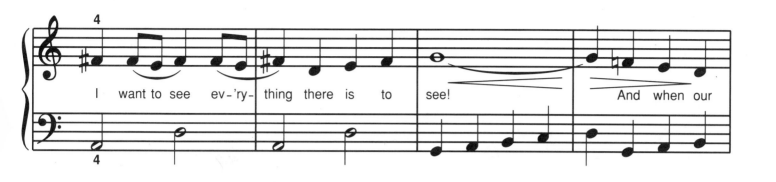

I want to see ev-'ry-thing there is to see! And when our

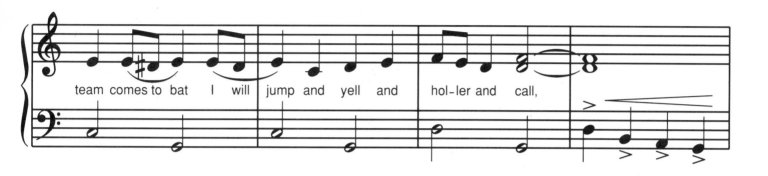

team comes to bat I will jump and yell and hol-ler and call,

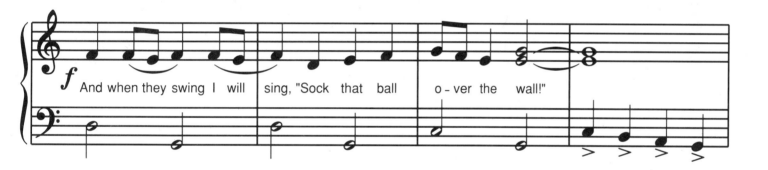

And when they swing I will sing, "Sock that ball o-ver the wall!"

Watch-ing a game is a lot of fun when our play-ers knock out a big home run, and

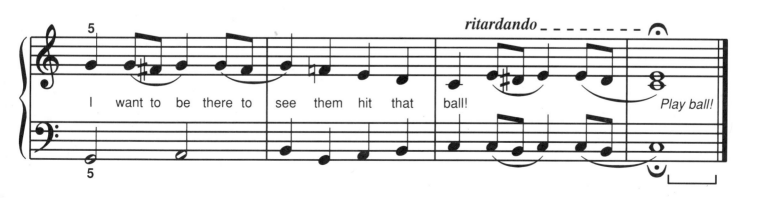

I want to be there to see them hit that ball! Play ball!

Use after SONATINA (page 68).

The Future Belongs to the Young

Moderately slow

sung, When all the old dreams are gone by. When

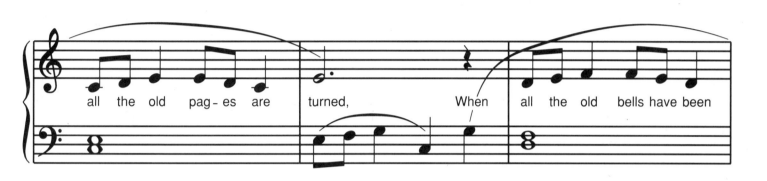

all the old pag - es are turned, When all the old bells have been

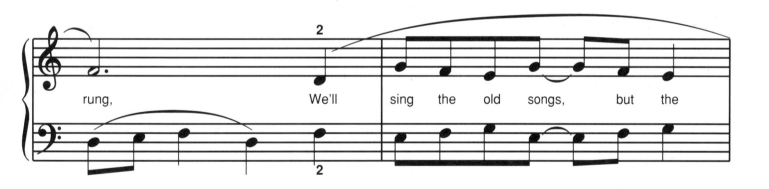

rung, We'll sing the old songs, but the

fu - ture be - longs to the young. *ritardando*

Ta-dah!

Use after SONATINA (page 68).

R.H. in C POSITION
L.H. in G POSITION

Allegro

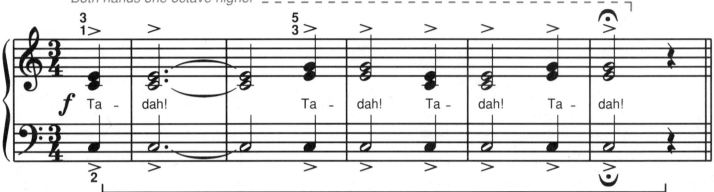

Both hands one octave higher

Ta - dah!   Ta - dah!   Ta - dah!   Ta - dah!

**With great pomp and power,
Not too slow!**

(R.H. as written)

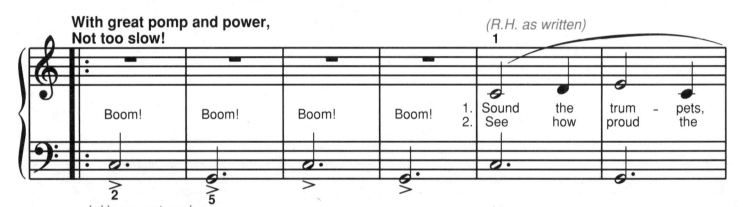

Boom!   Boom!   Boom!   Boom!   1. Sound the trum - pets,
2. See how proud the

L.H. one octave lower

here I come!   Ring the bells and   rat - tle the drum!
peo - ple look!   Shake my hand, I   fin - ished the book!

Both hands one octave higher

ritardando

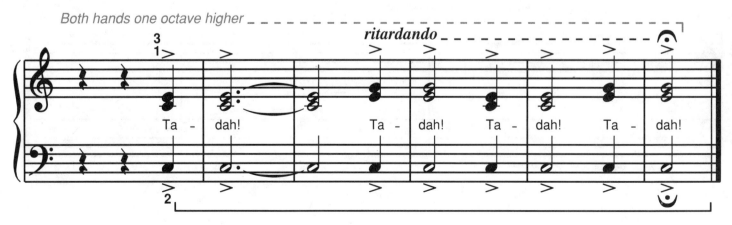

Ta - dah!   Ta - dah!   Ta - dah!   Ta - dah!